East Anglia

Edited By Lindsay Joyce

First published in Great Britain in 2018 by:

Young Writers
Remus House
Coltsfoot Drive
Peterborough
PE2 9BF
Telephone: 01733 890066
Website: www.youngwriters.co.uk

All Rights Reserved
Book Design by Ashley Janson
© Copyright Contributors 2017
SB ISBN 978-1-78896-092-2
Printed and bound in the UK by BookPrintingUK
Website: www.bookprintinguk.com
YB0345G

FOREWORD

Dear Reader,
Welcome to *Little Riddlers - East Anglia*, are you ready to get your thinking caps on to puzzle your way through this wonderful collection?

Young Writers' Little Riddlers competition set out to encourage young writers to create their own riddles. Their answers could be whatever or whoever their imaginations desired; from people to places, animals to objects, food to seasons. Riddles are a great way to further the children's use of poetic expression, including onomatopoeia and similes; as well as encourage them to 'think outside the box' by providing clues without giving the answer away immediately.

All of us at Young Writers believe in the importance of inspiring young children to produce creative writing, including poetry, and we feel that seeing their own riddles in print will keep that creative spirit burning brightly and proudly.

We hope you enjoy riddling your way through this book as much as we enjoyed reading all the entries.

CONTENTS

Aldeburgh Primary School, Aldeburgh

Agatha Battle (6)	1
Clementine Piers-Hall (5)	2
Freya Cook (5)	3
Henry George Bradley (6)	4
George Townsley (5)	5
Oliver Parish (6)	6
Kaci Parsons (5)	7

Corton Primary School, Corton

Poppy Stewart (6)	8
Cohen Corbett (6)	9
Emily Jenner (6)	10
Finlay Cassidy (6)	11
Gracie Gardner (6)	12
Freya Cudmore (5)	13
Kayley Cox (6)	14
Olivia Burrows (5)	15
Francesca Dale (6)	16
Oscar Fuller (5)	17
Ashton James Hart (7)	18
Isla Tabiner (5)	19
Summer Hood (6)	20
Ffion Bailey (5)	21
Mylo Gerrard Lake (5)	22
Ella Brooksbank (6)	23
Polly Jayne Jacobs (5)	24
Jenna Smith (6)	25
Madison Prue (5)	26

Eastfield Infant & Nursery School, St Ives

Tilly Podworska (6)	27
Bonnie Yorke (6)	28
Lillyane Mason (7)	29
Abigail Peak (6)	30
Oliver Frank Munns (6)	31
Toby Toseland (6)	32
Muhammad Dawood (5)	33
Aidan Megicks (6)	34
Millie Smith (6)	35
Sofia Palazzo (6)	36
Wafiq Ayan (5)	37
Gughan Prasanna (6)	38
Alicia Lawson (7)	39
Summer Bonny (7)	40
Lily Clifton (6)	41
Florence Deeprose (6)	42
Finley George Way (5)	43
Emily Turner (5)	44
Ava Gibson-Clubb (5)	45
Cailyn Thomas (6)	46
Adyan Khan (5)	47
Ayman Islam (5)	48
Molli Withers (6)	49
Jessica Louise Patterson (6)	50
Ana Doherty (5)	51
Edie Lewis (5)	52
Layla Burdett (5)	53
Annabel Horsfall Farman (5)	54
Freddie Pemberton (6)	55
Esme Abbott (6)	56
Juliana Harrisskitt (5)	57
Aaron Rivera (6)	58
Sebby Hill (5)	59

Oliver Ward (6)	60
Radha Madhurima Thotakura (6)	61
Inayah Adnan (6)	62
Shoaib Muhammad (5)	63
Kara-Elle Victoria Zirker (6)	64
Emma Phillips (7)	65
Luka Samuel Russell (5)	66
Aidan Wallbank (5)	67
Danny Simson (5)	68
Sienna Hall (5)	69
Joseph Eidt (6)	70
George Whitsey (5)	71
Cara Leigh-Brown (6)	72
Harry Williams (6)	73
Amelia Sutton (6)	74
Megan Rosier (6)	75
George Drummond (6)	76
Jack Morgan (6)	77
Haniya Fawad (6)	78
Skye Glover (6)	79
Aaliyah Ahmed (7)	80
Noah Austin (6)	81
Yele Mpakati (6)	82
Jazleen Kaur Singh (6)	83
Ralph Williams (6)	84
Alice Cridland (7)	85
Florence Golding (6)	86
Maddy Halliday (6)	87
Stanley Calverley (6)	88
Emily Howlieson (7)	89
Isabelle Abbott (5)	90
Amelie Holme (7)	91
Paige Rosier (6)	92
Alfie Loader (6)	93
Louis Powley (6)	94
Aaliyah Hawkins (5)	95
Freya Clark (6)	96
Jenson Peter Pauley (7)	97
Alex Perry (6)	98
Finley Ellinor (6)	99
Sam Schofield (7)	100
Archie Mace (6)	101
Imelda Townsend (6)	102
Evie Clark (6)	103
Austin Lailey (5)	104
Thomas Hird (5)	105
Logan Bateman (6)	106

Finborough School, Stowmarket

Finn Housden (6)	107
David Peck (6)	108
Freya Mills (6)	109
Artur Ronafoldi (6)	110
Izy Moody (7)	111
Rory Thomas Impett (6)	112
Alice Trebbick (6)	113
Sophie Beale (6)	114
Kismet Ersoy (6)	115
Murphy Wells (6)	116
Nathaniel Britton (6)	117
Ollie Sinclair (6)	118
Max Ryall (6)	119
Charlie Kavanagh (6)	120
Harrison Dore (6)	121
Damiano Di Miceli (6)	122
Adrian Pineda (6)	123
William Benterman (6)	124
Scarlett Liggett (7)	125
Jessica Hamilton (6)	126
Emilia Mayhew (6)	127
Bethan Redler (6)	128
Jack Mills (6)	129
Henry Castell (7)	130

Kennett Primary School, Kennett

Ollie Colbert (6)	131
James McAulay (6)	132
Jack Bevan (6)	133
Ellie Sheppard (6)	134
Maci Tricker (5)	135
Mikaeel Shujah (6)	136
Grace Ysobelle Taylor (6)	137
Wojtek Mickun (6)	138
Sammy French (6)	139

Harry Hetreed (6)	140
Evan Cornwell (6)	141
Tobias Cornwell (6)	142
Henry Watts (6)	143
Luke Lowe (5)	144
Lexie Mae Haird (5)	145
Joseph Smith (6)	146
Jessica Watson (5)	147
Harley King (6)	148
Henley Greenacre (6)	149
Danielle Mission (5)	150
Emily Crysell (5)	151
Harry Allison (5)	152
Chelsey Middleton (5)	153
Thea Tucker (5)	154
Jack Jones (5)	155
Tristan Edward Taylor (5)	156

Walpole Cross Keys Primary School, King's Lynn

Benjamin Eldridge (6)	157
Ella Mai Louise Ward (5)	158
Archie Munro (5)	159
Krystian Vancans (5)	160
Samuel Clements (7)	161

Wells Next The Sea Primary And Nursery, Wells-Next-The-Sea

Eliza Rosemary Wilson-Bell (7)	162
Ella-May Dawn Raven (6)	163
Alisha Beckham (6)	164
Lilly Andrews (6)	165
Kalei Dorothy Maisie Barnes (6)	166
Oska Somerton (6)	167
Edward Lees (7)	168
Ava-Jane Yaxley Beckham (6)	169
Ellie Duncan (6)	170
Daisy Rustom (6)	171
Zdennka Thomasine Gelder-Bailey (6)	172
Tilly Boulter (6)	173
Elise Honor Waajen (6)	174
Alfie George Thompson (6)	175
Isabelle Hayman (6)	176
Miguel Alexander Busque Pask (6)	177
Reece Steerment (6)	178

THE POEMS

What Am I?

I can be green and I'm not mean.
I live near a pond of which I am fond.
Jelly spawn I lay,
in which my young can play.
An amphibian I am,
can you guess what I am?
My feet are webbed.
I swim breaststroke and it's not a joke.
Do you know what I am?

Answer: A frog.

Agatha Battle (6)
Aldeburgh Primary School, Aldeburgh

Sneaky Thing!

I'm a spotty cat, fancy that!
I run faster than a cat
but can't go far.
Meat I eat which you can beat.
I have claws and teeth to eat my meat.
What am I?

Answer: A cheetah.

Clementine Piers-Hall (5)
Aldeburgh Primary School, Aldeburgh

Chatter Squawk

I have a strong beak.
I eat fresh fruit and nuts.
I have brightly-coloured feathers.
I can talk.
I can be a pet.
I live in a jungle or a cage.
What am I?

Answer: A parrot.

Freya Cook (5)
Aldeburgh Primary School, Aldeburgh

Guess Me, Smaller Than A Bee!

I am an insect you see.
Smaller than a bee.
I live in a nest and can be a pest.
I have six legs and hide my eggs.
My name rhymes with pant.
What am I?

Answer: An ant.

Henry George Bradley (6)
Aldeburgh Primary School, Aldeburgh

Prowling, Growling

I am a cat, fancy that, I hunt prey at night.
I live in the trees but you can't see me.
I have stripes on my fur and say 'grrr'.
What am I?

Answer: A tiger.

George Townsley (5)
Aldeburgh Primary School, Aldeburgh

Tickled Pink

I am pink and can stand in the drink.
I am pretty but I do not live in a city.
I am tall but I never fall.
What am I?

Answer: A flamingo.

Oliver Parish (6)
Aldeburgh Primary School, Aldeburgh

Cluck, Cluck, Good Luck

I live on a farm in a warm barn.
I have two legs and lay eggs.
I provide meat for you to eat.
What am I?

Answer: A chicken.

Kaci Parsons (5)
Aldeburgh Primary School, Aldeburgh

The Big, Fast Tiger

I run really fast like a racing car
My home is the jungle
My teeth are sharp and white
I hiss and roar when angry
I have lots of cubs
And teach them how to hunt
When they are dirty, I lick them clean,
Slurp, slurp, slurp!
My fur is stripy
I am orange like satsumas
And black as the night
What am I?

Answer: A tiger.

Poppy Stewart (6)
Corton Primary School, Corton

My Favourite Thing

I'm loved by all ages.
Boys and girls both enjoy me.
I come in all different colours.
You can build me into anything.
You can see me at a cinema.
You can see me at my own shop.
To build me follow the instructions
Or you can be creative.
I am the biggest selling toy in the world.
What am I?

Answer: Lego.

Cohen Corbett (6)
Corton Primary School, Corton

Bath Time Fun

I play with this for bath time fun.
In the bath it splashes my mum.
I have two wings but I can't fly.
When I'm around, you are never dry.
When I am in the bath I float
But I am not a boat.
I'm an animal that's made of plastic.
Emily thinks that I'm fantastic.
What am I?

Answer: A rubber duck.

Emily Jenner (6)
Corton Primary School, Corton

A Slimy Tale

I'm a little bit squidgy
And a little bit round.
Look out for the slime
I leave on the ground.
My eyes are on sticks
And my house is on my back.
Be gentle around me
Or my home may crack.
I wiggle like a worm
But I'm ever so slow.
If you catch me, let me go.
What am I?

Answer: A snail.

Finlay Cassidy (6)
Corton Primary School, Corton

My Best Friend

I like to play in the park.
I am hard to see in the dark.
I have a loud bark.
When I walk you can hear my claws clicking.
I like to give ears a good licking.
I like to chase a ball
And eat dinner with you all.
Wooden sticks I like to eat.
Gracie is my best friend.
What am I?

Answer: Winston, the dog.

Gracie Gardner (6)
Corton Primary School, Corton

Splash Splosh

I form on the ground
in a dip or a hollow.
I'm sometimes quite deep,
but can be quite shallow.
I'm filled by the clouds high in the sky.
Droplets of rain pitter-patter on my surface.
Water as murky as a swamp.
Drive, pedal or splash right through me.
What am I?

Answer: A puddle.

Freya Cudmore (5)
Corton Primary School, Corton

The Oldest Reptile

I don't move too well
And I live in a shell.
I have four small feet
And I have a beak.
I sleep for weeks and weeks.
When I'm hungry and need to feed
I like to eat weeds.
I come out in the sun
But winter is not fun.
What am I?

Answer: A tortoise.

Kayley Cox (6)
Corton Primary School, Corton

Yummy

My favourite food puts me in a good mood.
It is yummy in my tummy.
Normally cooked by my mummy.
You can dip it in sauce.
This tastes lovely of course.
The best topping is ham.
You could never have jam!
What is it?

Answer: A pizza.

Olivia Burrows (5)
Corton Primary School, Corton

Giddy Up!

I can run for miles
And jump high over stiles.
When wearing my tack
You can sit on my back.
My tail is long and straight,
I wave it at flies I hate.
I eat lots of hay,
To call my owner I neigh.
What am I?

Answer: A horse.

Francesca Dale (6)
Corton Primary School, Corton

Brick Building

I come in different shapes.
I stick together without tape.
Press me together and I click.
I'm a type of building brick.
I come in all colours of the rainbow.
You could even make the letter 'O'.
What am I?

Answer: Lego.

Oscar Fuller (5)
Corton Primary School, Corton

The Mysterious Animal

He has big fluffy paws
And walks through the jungle.
He runs fast,
Trying to find his dinner.
His roar is loud
As he plays with his cubs.
He eats meat.
Baby cubs sometimes eat smaller prey.
What is he?

Answer: A lion.

Ashton James Hart (7)
Corton Primary School, Corton

Fun In Winter

In summer I melt.
In winter I freeze.
I have sticks as arms
And buttons as eyes.
I am round like a ball
And as tall as you like.
I am as white as a polar bear
And as soft as cotton wool.
What am I?

Answer: A snowman.

Isla Tabiner (5)
Corton Primary School, Corton

My Soft Friend

I am not one size
And I don't eat pies.
I'm really fluffy
And also puffy.
I'm soft like a bunny,
Some of us like honey.
I like cuddles at bedtime.
Do you like my rhyme?
What am I?

Answer: A teddy bear.

Summer Hood (6)
Corton Primary School, Corton

What am I?

I'm big and brown
But soft as a feather.
In the summer I run around.
In the winter I sleep forever.
I have big claws on my paws.
If I'm around you should lock your doors.
What am I?

Answer: A bear.

Ffion Bailey (5)
Corton Primary School, Corton

Foot Fun

I'm as soft as a bear.
You can kick me in the air.
I'm as round as the sun.
I can be lots of fun.
You can aim for a goal
or you can even play alone.
What am I?

Answer: A football.

Mylo Gerrard Lake (5)
Corton Primary School, Corton

Jurassic Park

Their roar is loud,
Their stomps are proud.
They munch on greens,
They hunt in teams.
If you look up high
You'll also see them in the sky.
What are they?

Answer: Dinosaurs.

Ella Brooksbank (6)
Corton Primary School, Corton

Pretty Seeds

We plant the seeds
We need the sun
Get some water
Run, run, run
Lots of bees and colours too
Purple, pink, golden and blue
I cannot wait to show you
What am I?

Answer: A flower.

Polly Jayne Jacobs (5)
Corton Primary School, Corton

Fake Cake

I come in a tub.
If you drop me I'll thud.
Squish it, shape it,
Roll it, make it.
I create beautiful cakes.
What cakes would you make?
What am I?

Answer: Play-Doh.

Jenna Smith (6)
Corton Primary School, Corton

Here Kitty Kitty

She crawls slowly.
She is super speedy.
She has sharp claws and big teeth.
She has a lovely spotty coat.
What is she?

Answer: A leopard. (upside down)

Madison Prue (5)
Corton Primary School, Corton

Little Riddlers - East Anglia

Guess Who...

My eyes are as blue as the lines in the book.
I'm a girl.
I'm an owl but I have no wings.
I'm taller than a shoe.
My hair is as brown as wood.
I'm smaller than a horse.
I like to play with my eleven pets.
I'm seven next year.
I'm in Year 2.
I'm writing with my right hand at the moment.
Who am I?

Answer: Tilly.

Tilly Podworska (6)
Eastfield Infant & Nursery School, St Ives

Hey You!

I am a lovely child.
I am taller than a wavy plant.
I am smaller than a big, leafy tree.
I am as tall as my kitten.
My hair is curly, short and golden brown.
My eyes are light blue like the sky.
My name starts with the letter 'B'.
I like my fluffy, cheeky baby kittens.
Who am I?

Answer: Bonnie.

Bonnie Yorke (6)
Eastfield Infant & Nursery School, St Ives

Guess Who I Am

I am an owl but have no wings.
I am a girl.
I am as nice as Cinderella.
I like to sing and dance.
I like pizza.
My eyes are as blue as blueberries.
My hair is as blonde as the stars.
I am amazing!
I am really sweet.
I am seven years old.
I am an owl.
Who am I?

Answer: Lillyanne.

Lillyane Mason (7)
Eastfield Infant & Nursery School, St Ives

Who Am I?

My name starts with an 'A'.
I am a girl.
My eyes are as green as a leaf.
I love playing with my toys.
My skin is a pinky colour.
I like eating party food.
I am smaller than a tree.
I like going to school.
I also like doing homework.
I like to dream.
Who am I?

Answer: Abigail.

Abigail Peak (6)
Eastfield Infant & Nursery School, St Ives

Guess Who?

My hair is as brown as mud.
I am a boy.
I am taller than a baby.
I like playing.
I have peach skin.
I like chocolate.
I am taller than a chair.
My name starts with an 'O'.
I am six years old.
I have two eyes.
My eyes are as blue as the sea.
Who am I?

Answer: Oliver.

Oliver Frank Munns (6)
Eastfield Infant & Nursery School, St Ives

Name That Riddle

What am I?
You can grow me.
I am as fat as a football.
I come in different shapes and sizes.
I am orange or yellow.
My stalk is a different colour to my body.
You get me at Halloween.
I grow on a patch.
You carve me.
I am a type of vegetable.
What am I?

Answer: A pumpkin.

Toby Toseland (6)
Eastfield Infant & Nursery School, St Ives

Little Riddlers - East Anglia

Hey You!

I am a person.
I am taller than my brothers.
I am smaller than a tall giraffe.
I am as fast as a cheetah.
My hair is black.
My eyes are brown.
My name begins with the letter 'D'.
I like my friend, Wafiq.
Who am I?

Answer: Dawood.

Muhammad Dawood (5)
Eastfield Infant & Nursery School, St Ives

Tasty Treat

I have no legs.
I am alive.
I could be red or green.
I am tasty for your tummy.
You can find me on a tree.
I will be a big treat.
I have a little stick out of my top.
What am I?

Answer: An apple.

Aidan Megicks (6)
Eastfield Infant & Nursery School, St Ives

What Do You Think I Am?

I don't breathe.
People stick things in me.
I have a cupboard.
I have windows and doors.
I sometimes have a pointy roof
or a flat roof.
Children learn in me.
What am I?

Answer: A school classroom.

Millie Smith (6)
Eastfield Infant & Nursery School, St Ives

Jungle Animals

I walk slow.
I have two legs and two arms.
I'm slow and I climb in trees.
I like to eat.
I'm soft.
I have white paws.
I have four legs.
I am black and white.
What am I?

Answer: A panda.

Sofia Palazzo (6)
Eastfield Infant & Nursery School, St Ives

Hey You!

I am a human.
I am shorter than a long giraffe.
I am taller than tiny ants.
I am smaller than Titanic.
I am as cheeky as a monkey.
My hair is black.
My eyes are brown.
Who am I?

Answer: Wafiq.

Wafiq Ayan (5)
Eastfield Infant & Nursery School, St Ives

Bendy

I am tall like a tower.
I sometimes don't work.
I've got a door.
I am wide.
I've got something long.
I use wind to work.
I'm sometimes in water.
What am I?

Answer: A wind turbine.

Gughan Prasanna (6)
Eastfield Infant & Nursery School, St Ives

Who Am I?

I am an owl
Without any wings.
My hair is blonde and straight.
I am a girl.
I have a dog named Honey.
My favourite dinner is spaghetti bolognese.
I love chocolate cake.
Who am I?

Answer: Alicia.

Alicia Lawson (7)
Eastfield Infant & Nursery School, St Ives

What Am I?

You can lay in me.
You can relax in me.
You can play in me.
You can put hot and cold water in me.
You can splash in me.
You can put soap in me
And I will bubble up.
What am I?

Answer: A bath.

Summer Bonny (7)
Eastfield Infant & Nursery School, St Ives

Guess Who?

I am taller than a baby.
I am a girl.
I am shorter than an adult.
My eyes are blue.
I like playing outside.
I am an owl but I have no wings.
My hair is long.
Who am I?

Answer: Lily.

Lily Clifton (6)
Eastfield Infant & Nursery School, St Ives

Who Am I?

My eyes are blue.
I am an owl but I have no wings.
I am a girl.
My hair is blonde.
I am taller than a cat.
I am shorter than a giraffe.
I like spaghetti.
Who am I?

Answer: Flo D.

Florence Deeprose (6)
Eastfield Infant & Nursery School, St Ives

Who Am I?

My hair is blonde.
I am a boy.
I am an owl but I have no wings.
My eyes are blue.
I am taller than a chair.
I like pie.
I am shorter than an adult.
Who am I?

Answer: *Finley Way.*

Finley George Way (5)
Eastfield Infant & Nursery School, St Ives

Hey You!

I am as fast as a cheetah.
I am smaller than a small giraffe.
I like my mummy.
My hair is soft.
My eyes are blue.
My name starts with the letter 'E'.
Who am I?

Answer: Emily.

Emily Turner (5)
Eastfield Infant & Nursery School, St Ives

Little Riddlers - East Anglia

Hey You!

I am a person.
I am taller than a mouse.
I am as loud as a dinosaur.
My hair is long and golden.
My eyes are like the sky.
My name starts with an 'A'.
Who am I?

Answer: Ava.

Ava Gibson-Clubb (5)
Eastfield Infant & Nursery School, St Ives

Hey You!

My eyes are brown.
My name starts with the letter 'C'.
I like my brother.
I go to the park.
I am smaller than a tree.
I am as funny as an elephant.
Who am I?

Answer: Cailyn.

Cailyn Thomas (6)
Eastfield Infant & Nursery School, St Ives

Hey You!

I am a boy.
I am taller than a bug.
I am a hedgehog but I have no spikes.
My hair is short.
I like police cars.
My name begins with the letter 'A'.
Who am I?

Answer: Adyan.

Adyan Khan (5)
Eastfield Infant & Nursery School, St Ives

Hey You!

I am a person.
I am taller than my sister.
I am smaller than a big giraffe.
My hair is short and black.
My eyes are brown.
I like to play with my friends.
Who am I?

Answer: Ayman.

Ayman Islam (5)
Eastfield Infant & Nursery School, St Ives

Hey You!

My eyes are brown.
My name starts with the letter 'M'.
I like kittens.
I am smaller than an elephant.
I go to town.
I am as happy as the sun.
Who am I?

Answer: Molli.

Molli Withers (6)
Eastfield Infant & Nursery School, St Ives

Guess Who...

I am an owl with no wings.
I am a girl and I am kind.
My hair is long and straight
And it is as blonde as the sun.
I wear my hair down.
I am in Year 2.
Who am I?

Answer: Jessica.

Jessica Louise Patterson (6)
Eastfield Infant & Nursery School, St Ives

Hey You!

I am a person.
I am taller than a spotty dog.
I am smaller than a house.
My hair is shiny and golden.
My eyes are blue, like the sun.
I like strawberries.
Who am I?

Answer: Ana.

Ana Doherty (5)
Eastfield Infant & Nursery School, St Ives

Hey You!

I am as fast as a cheetah.
I like monkeys.
I am smaller than a grown-up.
My eyes are blue.
My hair is blonde.
My name starts with the letter 'E'.
Who am I?

Answer: Edie.

Edie Lewis (5)
Eastfield Infant & Nursery School, St Ives

Hey You!

I am as funny as a clown.
I am smaller than an elephant.
I like my dogs.
I go to the park.
My eyes are blue.
My name starts with the letter 'L'.
Who am I?

Answer: Layla.

Layla Burdett (5)
Eastfield Infant & Nursery School, St Ives

Who Am I?

I am a girl.
I am taller than my baby.
My eyes are blue.
I am an owl but I have no wings.
I am shorter than my mummy.
I like to play with my friends.
Who am I?

Answer: Annabel.

Annabel Horsfall Farman (5)
Eastfield Infant & Nursery School, St Ives

What Am I?

I have scaly skin.
I have sharp teeth.
I have sharp claws.
I have three claws on each foot.
I have over forty teeth.
I have very big claws.
What am I?

Answer: A dinosaur.

Freddie Pemberton (6)
Eastfield Infant & Nursery School, St Ives

What Am I?

I have four legs.
I cannot live somewhere frozen.
I can run fast and I live in the jungle.
I am a type of cat.
I eat meat.
I have stripy fur.
What am I?

Answer: A tiger.

Esme Abbott (6)
Eastfield Infant & Nursery School, St Ives

Hey You!

I am as sleepy as a hedgehog.
I am smaller than a grown-up.
I go to the toy shops.
My name starts with the letter 'J'.
My eyes are brown.
Who am I?

Answer: Juliana.

Juliana Harrisskitt (5)
Eastfield Infant & Nursery School, St Ives

Guess Who?

My eyes are brown like a horse.
My name starts with an 'A'.
My favourite pudding is ice cream.
My hair is as black as the dark.
I am a boy.
Who am I?

Answer: Aaron.

Aaron Rivera (6)
Eastfield Infant & Nursery School, St Ives

Hey You!

I am a boy.
I am taller than my nanny.
I am a hedgehog.
My name starts with the letter 'S'.
My hair is a bit golden.
I like football.
Who am I?

Answer: Sebby.

Sebby Hill (5)
Eastfield Infant & Nursery School, St Ives

Guess The Riddle

You can grow me.
You don't see me about.
I need water to live.
I don't swim in water.
I am green all the way around.
Pandas eat me.
What am I?

Answer: Bamboo.

Oliver Ward (6)
Eastfield Infant & Nursery School, St Ives

Reindeer

My fur is brown.
I eat carrots.
I have a red nose.
I fly with Santa.
I live in the North Pole.
I have four legs.
Who am I?

Answer: Rudolph the red-nosed reindeer.

Radha Madhurima Thotakura (6)
Eastfield Infant & Nursery School, St Ives

Hey You!

I am a kind person.
I am taller than sticky glue.
I am smaller than a brick house.
My hair is black.
My eyes are brown.
I like pancakes.
Who am I?

Answer: Inayah.

Inayah Adnan (6)
Eastfield Infant & Nursery School, St Ives

Hey You!

I am a person.
I am taller than a dog.
I am smaller than flowers.
My hair is short and black.
My eyes are brown.
I like gold lollipops.
Who am I?

Answer: Shoaib.

Shoaib Muhammad (5)
Eastfield Infant & Nursery School, St Ives

River Animal

I am brown.
I can't fly.
I can live in lakes too.
I can swim very fast.
My name starts with 'O'.
I have four legs.
What am I?

Answer: A river otter.

Kara-Elle Victoria Zirker (6)
Eastfield Infant & Nursery School, St Ives

What Am I?

I am hairy.
I am dangerous.
I live in the desert.
I live in a hole.
I am black and orange.
I am scary.
I have eight legs.
What am I?

Answer: A tarantula.

Emma Phillips (7)
Eastfield Infant & Nursery School, St Ives

Hey You!

My hair is brown.
My eyes are green.
I go to football.
I have a pet dog
And he plays football too.
My name starts with an 'L'.
Who am I?

Answer: Luka.

Luka Samuel Russell (5)
Eastfield Infant & Nursery School, St Ives

Hey You!

I am a person.
I am taller than my cat.
I am smaller than my dad.
I am as tall as a tent.
My hair is curly.
I like watching videos.
Who am I?

Answer: Aidan.

Aidan Wallbank (5)
Eastfield Infant & Nursery School, St Ives

Hey You!

I am a person.
I am taller than a bug.
I am smaller than a house.
My hair is short and brown.
My eyes are brown.
I like bubblegum.
Who am I?

Answer: Danny.

Danny Simson (5)
Eastfield Infant & Nursery School, St Ives

Hey You!

I am a person.
I am taller than a cat.
I am smaller than my friend, Alayna.
My hair is blonde.
My eyes are blue.
I like my cat.
Who am I?

Answer: Sienna.

Sienna Hall (5)
Eastfield Infant & Nursery School, St Ives

A Long Time Ago

I lived a long time ago.
I have feathers but I can't fly.
I lived on an island.
I was hunted by humans.
I am not very big.
What am I?

Answer: A dodo bird.

Joseph Eidt (6)
Eastfield Infant & Nursery School, St Ives

Hey You!

I am a person.
I am taller than my sister.
I am smaller than my mum.
My hair is blonde.
My eyes are green.
I like watching TV.
Who am I?

Answer: George.

George Whitsey (5)
Eastfield Infant & Nursery School, St Ives

Name Me

I have four legs.
I am not a person but I am alive.
I am sometimes as light as a feather.
My nose is wet and I go *woof, woof!*
What am I?

Answer: A dog.

Cara Leigh-Brown (6)
Eastfield Infant & Nursery School, St Ives

What Am I?

I am big.
I'm scary at night.
You put fire inside me.
I come from a farm.
I am orange.
You cut me.
You eat me.
What am I?

Answer: A pumpkin.

Harry Williams (6)
Eastfield Infant & Nursery School, St Ives

Crunchy

I am a sort of vegetable.
You can grow me.
I have no legs or arms.
I grow in soil.
I have green on the top.
I am orange.
What am I?

Answer: A carrot.

Amelia Sutton (6)
Eastfield Infant & Nursery School, St Ives

What Am I?

I am black and white.
I am as soft as a teddy.
I am cute.
I have patches on my eyes.
I come from China.
I eat bamboo.
What am I?

Answer: A panda.

Megan Rosier (6)
Eastfield Infant & Nursery School, St Ives

Vehicles

I come in different colours.
I have wheels.
I have windows.
I fit on rails.
I stop at every station.
I am not alive.
What am I?

Answer: A train.

George Drummond (6)
Eastfield Infant & Nursery School, St Ives

Guess What The Riddle Is?

I have four legs
But I can't climb up trees.
I come in different colours.
People ride me.
I say, 'Neigh!'
What am I?

Answer: A horse.

Jack Morgan (6)
Eastfield Infant & Nursery School, St Ives

Look In My Garden

I am a vegetable.
I look like a finger.
I am crunchy.
I feel so bumpy.
Rabbits like to eat me.
I am orange.
What am I?

Answer: A carrot.

Haniya Fawad (6)
Eastfield Infant & Nursery School, St Ives

What Am I?

I have feathers.
I am soft.
I like eating bread.
I like to swim in the pond.
I have wings and I can fly.
What am I?

Answer: A duck.

Skye Glover (6)
Eastfield Infant & Nursery School, St Ives

What Does A Riddle Need?

I have eight legs.
I live in the sea.
I have ten tentacles.
I am alive in the Atlantic.
I am not a fish.
What am I?

Answer: An octopus.

Aaliyah Ahmed (7)
Eastfield Infant & Nursery School, St Ives

Slow!

I live in the jungle.
I am slow.
I climb trees.
I have long sharp nails.
I have two legs.
I am free.
What am I?

Answer: A sloth.

Noah Austin (6)
Eastfield Infant & Nursery School, St Ives

Guess Who?

I am a girl with short hair.
I like to sing.
I go to school.
My name starts with 'Y'.
I am in Year 2.
Who am I?

Answer: Yele.

Yele Mpakati (6)
Eastfield Infant & Nursery School, St Ives

Hey You!

My hair is blonde.
My eyes are brown.
I like to swim.
I am taller than ants.
I enjoy playing with my toys.
Who am I?

Answer: Jazleen.

Jazleen Kaur Singh (6)
Eastfield Infant & Nursery School, St Ives

Guess The Thing

I lived a long time ago.
I am extinct.
I come in different sizes.
I can fly.
I have pointy wings.
What am I?

Answer: A pterodactyl.

Ralph Williams (6)
Eastfield Infant & Nursery School, St Ives

Grey Or Brown

I have grey or brown skin.
I like climbing.
I live in trees.
I love nuts.
I have a big bushy tail.
What am I?

Answer: A squirrel.

Alice Cridland (7)
Eastfield Infant & Nursery School, St Ives

Guess Who?

I am a girl.
I have brown hair.
My eyes are as blue as the sky.
I like playing with my friends.
Who am I?

Answer: Florence Golding.

Florence Golding (6)
Eastfield Infant & Nursery School, St Ives

What Am I?

I am white.
I am cold.
I can be big or little.
You can build me.
I have a carrot for a nose.
What am I?

Answer: A snowman.

Maddy Halliday (6)
Eastfield Infant & Nursery School, St Ives

A Flying Animal

I am black.
I am soft and I have a big beak.
I am also big and have lots of feathers.
I can fly.
What am I?

Answer: A raven.

Stanley Calverley (6)
Eastfield Infant & Nursery School, St Ives

I Like Cats

I like to climb trees.
I don't like to get wet.
I like to drink water.
I like to be hugged.
What am I?

Answer: A cat.

Emily Howlieson (7)
Eastfield Infant & Nursery School, St Ives

Guess Who?

I have brown hair.
I am a girl.
I like jumping in puddles.
I am five.
My skin is white.
Who am I?

Answer: Isabelle.

Isabelle Abbott (5)
Eastfield Infant & Nursery School, St Ives

Guess Who?

I am an owl but I have no wings.
My hair is as red as fire.
My eyes are as hazel as hazelnuts.
Who am I?

Answer: Amelie.

Amelie Holme (7)
Eastfield Infant & Nursery School, St Ives

What Am I?

I'm hard.
I'm white.
You can play with me.
I'm round like a trampoline.
What am I?

Answer: A football.

Paige Rosier (6)
Eastfield Infant & Nursery School, St Ives

What Am I?

I am small.
I have a red and green shirt.
I am with Santa
And I live in the North Pole.
Who am I?

Answer: An elf.

Alfie Loader (6)
Eastfield Infant & Nursery School, St Ives

What Am I?

I live in a dark habitat.
I don't shave or wash.
I live in a spooky cave.
Who am I?

Answer: Caveman Dave.

Louis Powley (6)
Eastfield Infant & Nursery School, St Ives

Hey You!

My hair is black.
My eyes are black.
I like to swim.
I am taller than a hedgehog.
Who am I?

Answer: Aaliyah.

Aaliyah Hawkins (5)
Eastfield Infant & Nursery School, St Ives

What Am I?

I have two legs.
I have two arms.
I am cheeky.
I live in the wet, green jungle.
What am I?

Answer: A monkey.

Freya Clark (6)
Eastfield Infant & Nursery School, St Ives

What Am I?

I am fast.
I am camouflaged.
I live in a tree.
I have wings.
What am I?

Answer: A peregrine falcon.

Jenson Peter Pauley (7)
Eastfield Infant & Nursery School, St Ives

What Am I?

I have four legs.
I am not alive.
I don't walk.
You sit in me.
What am I?

Answer: A chair.

Alex Perry (6)
Eastfield Infant & Nursery School, St Ives

Stripy

I have claws as sharp as razors.
I run very fast.
I live in the jungle.
What am I?

Answer: A tiger.

Finley Ellinor (6)
Eastfield Infant & Nursery School, St Ives

Guess Who I Am?

I am a boy.
I am in Owl Class.
I like cake.
I have two best friends.
Who am I?

Answer: Sammy.

Sam Schofield (7)
Eastfield Infant & Nursery School, St Ives

What Am I?

I am black.
I have six legs.
I go in the grass.
I eat leaves.
What am I?

Answer: An ant.

Archie Mace (6)
Eastfield Infant & Nursery School, St Ives

Cheeky

I am brown and furry.
I love to climb trees
And I love bananas.
What am I?

Answer: A monkey.

Imelda Townsend (6)
Eastfield Infant & Nursery School, St Ives

Write Us A Riddle

I can fly and I am red.
I am fast.
I have black spots.
What am I?

Answer: A ladybird.

Evie Clark (6)
Eastfield Infant & Nursery School, St Ives

Guess Who?

I am a boy.
I am bigger than a mouse.
I have brown hair.
Who am I?

Answer: Austin.

Austin Lailey (5)
Eastfield Infant & Nursery School, St Ives

Hey You!

My hair is blonde.
My eyes are blue.
I go to the park.
Who am I?

Answer: Thomas.

Thomas Hird (5)
Eastfield Infant & Nursery School, St Ives

What Am I?

I have four legs.
I am sometimes stripy.
I eat meat.
What am I?

Answer: A tiger.

Logan Bateman (6)
Eastfield Infant & Nursery School, St Ives

Get Ready To Munch

I live in a packet and I'm very yummy.
I'm not alive.
Dogs like munching on me.
I have five fingers.
I have a hole in the middle of me.
People like eating me too.
I have lots of very scrummy friends.
I am as yellow as some cheese.
I am spiky to eat.
I'm a monster but I don't roar.
What am I?

Answer: Monster Munch.

Finn Housden (6)
Finborough School, Stowmarket

Guess Quiz!

I have a stripy body.
I like to eat meat.
I have sharp teeth.
I live in the desert.
I'm spooky.
I'm really fast.
I have black eyes.
I have claws.
I'm as scary as a lion.
I'm as scary as a disgusting, horrible zombie.
What am I?

Answer: A tiger.

David Peck (6)
Finborough School, Stowmarket

Run Run As Fast As You Can!

I live up high in a mountain.
I am sometimes grey or red.
I sometimes steal food from people like a thief.
I have a long curly tail like a donkey.
I am faster than a horse.
I have hands but I can't clap.
I have eyes as black as obsidian.
What am I?

Answer: A squirrel.

Freya Mills (6)
Finborough School, Stowmarket

Always Jump To The Sky!

I live in huge USA.
I am as rich as the Queen.
I live in medium Cleveland.
I am stronger than a lion.
Maybe next year I will live
in shiny Los Angeles.
I am faster than a cheetah.
I can jump as high as the sky.
Who am I?

Answer: LeBron James.

Artur Ronafoldi (6)
Finborough School, Stowmarket

The Craziest Riddle Ever!

I can do lots of stuff at once.
I am as slimy as a slug.
I can blend in with stuff.
I live underwater.
I can be as orange as a basketball.
I love finding stuff.
I squirt black ink.
What am I?

Answer: A squid.

Izy Moody (7)
Finborough School, Stowmarket

Power Walk

You will never lose me.
I cannot see.
I am as black as oblivion.
I can walk.
I can swim like a shark.
I am as fast as a cheetah.
I can follow a bird everywhere.
What am I?

Answer: A shadow.

Rory Thomas Impett (6)
Finborough School, Stowmarket

Who Has Beady Eyes?

I can see a long way from here.
I have a tail as long as a snake.
I am as fast as a shark.
I look at you with my beady eyes.
I have a favourite food, it's very crunchy.
What am I?

Answer: A squirrel.

Alice Trebbick (6)
Finborough School, Stowmarket

The Great Riddle

I'm as beautiful as a rainbow.
I have big eyes.
I'm as wild as a lion.
I have four legs.
I love running.
You have to clean me out every day.
I like carrots.
What am I?

Answer: A horse.

Sophie Beale (6)
Finborough School, Stowmarket

The Big Job

I am as beautiful as a rainbow.
I am as amazing as a lion.
I look very yellow.
I have four legs.
I am very strange.
I am a tall animal.
I am seen everywhere.
What am I?

Answer: A giraffe.

Kismet Ersoy (6)
Finborough School, Stowmarket

The Trickiest Trick

I am as tall as a trap.
I am as sloppy as a slope.
I am as brave as a knight.
I am as fast as a cheetah.
I am as free as a lion.
I am as black as ink.
What am I?

Answer: A panther.

Murphy Wells (6)
Finborough School, Stowmarket

The Best Riddle

I am a captain.
I am as strong as The Hulk.
I am as powerful as a superhero.
I am as fast as a cheetah.
I am always kind.
I have a round shield.
Who am I?

Answer: Captain America.

Nathaniel Britton (6)
Finborough School, Stowmarket

The Eater

I have black and white fur.
I eat meat.
I am a meat eater.
I hunt as a pack.
I have a massive tail.
I live in the desert.
I am as fast as a lion.
What am I?

Answer: A hyena.

Ollie Sinclair (6)
Finborough School, Stowmarket

The Challenge Of Doom!

My fur is as soft as a cushion.
My beak is as sharp as a nail.
My legs are long and grown-up.
My eyes are as big as cows.
My eggs are as cute as babies.
What am I?

Answer: An ostrich.

Max Ryall (6)
Finborough School, Stowmarket

The Awesome Riddle

I am as grey as a rhino.
I am as fast as a cheetah.
I live in unusual places.
I can blend in.
You will find me in dirty places.
I am grey or brown.
What am I?

Answer: A mouse.

Charlie Kavanagh (6)
Finborough School, Stowmarket

Great Animals

I have teeth as sharp as mountains.
I am very spotty.
I am as fast as a rocket.
I like to eat prey.
I love to run very fast.
I am really scary.
What am I?

Answer: A cheetah.

Harrison Dore (6)
Finborough School, Stowmarket

Ticking Speed

I can't clap
But I do have hands.
Some people look at me.
I do not have batteries.
I am as big as 90 millimetres.
I sometimes go away.
What am I?

Answer: A clock.

Damiano Di Miceli (6)
Finborough School, Stowmarket

The Famous Riddle

I have scary, dark purple skin.
I have two legs.
I like the dark.
I am scary.
I fly.
I have wings.
I fly as fast as an aeroplane.
What am I?

Answer: A bat.

Adrian Pineda (6)
Finborough School, Stowmarket

The Amazing Riddle

I have wheels.
I'm as fast as a cheetah.
I am big or small.
I can go on a track.
I am as fun as school.
I can be dangerous.
What am I?

Answer: A skateboard.

William Benterman (6)
Finborough School, Stowmarket

Sweet Cakes

I am a cat but as sweet
as honey and lavender.
I have no hair but I'm feline.
I am crunchy as crisps.
I am better than vegetables.
What am I?

Answer: A kitkat.

Scarlett Liggett (7)
Finborough School, Stowmarket

The Challenge

I love the dark.
I have a beak.
I have big wings.
I live in the tall trees.
I have jewelled eyes.
I have spotty, soft feathers.
What am I?

Answer: An owl.

Jessica Hamilton (6)
Finborough School, Stowmarket

Fly, Fly

I am as fast as a bird.
I am very sweet.
I have two legs.
I have two beautiful eyes.
I fly silently like a person sleeping.
What am I?

Answer: An owl.

Emilia Mayhew (6)
Finborough School, Stowmarket

Speedy

I am black and white.
I live in a house.
I have an owner.
I have a bed.
I have a toy.
I have paws.
What am I?

Answer: A dog.

Bethan Redler (6)
Finborough School, Stowmarket

A Great Mystery

I run fast.
I have long legs.
I have little ears.
I like to eat grass.
I have stripes.
What am I?

Answer: A zebra.

Jack Mills (6)
Finborough School, Stowmarket

Undersea Biter

I am deadlier than poison.
I live down under.
I have crushing teeth.
What am I?

Answer: A shark.

Henry Castell (7)
Finborough School, Stowmarket

Grass Swimmers

I have a scaly body like a fish.
I weave my way through the long grass.
I have a red tongue and I live
in North America.
People freeze when they hear my rattle.
My poisonous bite makes people die.
I'm as scratchy as sandpaper.
I slither silently across the ground.
What am I?

Answer: A rattlesnake.

Ollie Colbert (6)
Kennett Primary School, Kennett

Night Hunter

I'm as spooky as a ghost.
I live in the dark, cold woodlands.
I have big, dark, spooky eyes.
I have big grey feathers.
I have pointy, sharp talons.
My sharp beak pecks on tree logs.
I have huge, orange feet.
I glide silently through the dark,
cold woodlands.
What am I?

Answer: An owl.

James McAulay (6)
Kennett Primary School, Kennett

The Blood Crusher

I eat things as shiny as garden tools.
I live in the tropical sea.
My skin is shinier than a sink.
I'm super duper fast
as I proceed through the water.
My teeth are razor-sharp like knives.
I also surround things like whirlpools.
What am I?

Answer: A barracuda.

Jack Bevan (6)
Kennett Primary School, Kennett

High Diver

I'm as graceful as a mermaid.
I'm a sea creature like a shark.
You can hear me laughing while I catch fish.
I'm as squeaky as a mouse.
I'm as quick as lightning.
I'm a mermaid's friend.
What am I?

Answer: A dolphin.

Ellie Sheppard (6)
Kennett Primary School, Kennett

African Skyscraper

I have yellow and black spots
all over my skin.
I am as tall as a skyscraper.
I eat leaves with my long black tongue.
I am graceful when I run.
My neck is as long as a tree.
My eyes are as black as coal.
What am I?

Answer: A giraffe.

Maci Tricker (5)
Kennett Primary School, Kennett

The High African Bus

I have thick, grey skin all over my body.
I have a long, sharp horn.
I have a really fat tummy.
I'm as heavy as a lorry.
I stomp louder than a giant.
My skin is as dry as the ground I stand on.
What am I?

Answer: A rhino.

Mikaeel Shujah (6)
Kennett Primary School, Kennett

Stomper

I have stomping, heavy, grey feet.
My skin is as hard as a rock.
I'm as heavy as a truck.
I live in Africa.
I have a big, sharp horn
that fights every animal.
I'm as mad as a monkey.
What am I?

Answer: A rhino.

Grace Ysobelle Taylor (6)
Kennett Primary School, Kennett

What Am I?

I have massive wings.
I can fly as high as a mountain.
I'm the symbol of North America.
I love to gobble up meat.
I have big claws, as sharp as a razor.
I have a humongous head.
What am I?

Answer: An eagle.

Wojtek Mickun (6)
Kennett Primary School, Kennett

The Biter

I hunt for juicy meat.
My teeth are as sharp as metal.
I'm as fluffy as a teddy bear.
I have colourful stripes.
My feet are as soft as a polar bear.
I growl as loud as a cheetah.
What am I?

Answer: A *tiger*.

Sammy French (6)
Kennett Primary School, Kennett

The Growl

I have sharp teeth like a thorn.
I live in Africa.
My mane is as fluffy as a teddy bear.
I prowl in the long grass like a cat.
My feet are fluffy.
My roar is as loud as a tiger.
What am I?

Answer: A lion.

Harry Hetreed (6)
Kennett Primary School, Kennett

Killer Of The Sea

I have sharp teeth.
I have a long tail.
I glide through the sea.
My skin is dark blue.
I have small, beady eyes.
I stalk my prey in the sea.
Fishermen are scared of me.
What am I?

Answer: A shark.

Evan Cornwell (6)
Kennett Primary School, Kennett

Colourful Fellow

I live in the desert.
I'm as small as a baby tiger.
I have green, rough skin.
On the sand my claws go *scratch!*
I have very small eyes.
I have a very long tail.
What am I?

Answer: A lizard.

Tobias Cornwell (6)
Kennett Primary School, Kennett

I Run Fast

I am as fast as a dog.
I have dark black spots.
I am as soft as a pillow.
I can climb trees and I eat meat.
I have yellow skin and black spots.
I have very sharp claws.
What am I?

Answer: A cheetah.

Henry Watts (6)
Kennett Primary School, Kennett

The Fastest Runner

I am as soft as a pillow.
I hunt for juicy meat.
I have spots all over me.
I live in the African grasslands.
My claws are as sharp as a knife.
I am as fast as the wind.
What am I?

Answer: A cheetah.

Luke Lowe (5)
Kennett Primary School, Kennett

Long Neck

I eat green leaves.
I have a long neck.
I have long yellow ears.
My feet stomp and it goes *tap, tap!*
I am as tall as trees.
My spots are like a Dalmatian.
What am I?

Answer: A giraffe.

Lexie Mae Haird (5)
Kennett Primary School, Kennett

The Tree Climber

I'm as furry as a gorilla.
I swing from tree to tree.
I have a long tail.
I have sharp teeth.
I eat plants from trees.
I'm as soft as cotton wool.
What am I?

Answer: A monkey.

Joseph Smith (6)
Kennett Primary School, Kennett

Stomp

I have sharp teeth.
My skin is red.
I eat apples.
I am as big as a tree.
I eat leaves and plants.
I make a loud roar.
My feet stomp on the ground.
What am I?

Answer: A dinosaur.

Jessica Watson (5)
Kennett Primary School, Kennett

Running Walker

I live in Africa.
My skin is crackled and grey.
My skin is like the moon.
My horn is shiny.
I'm high up like a bus.
My toenails are as big as a mouse.
What am I?

Answer: A rhino.

Harley King (6)
Kennett Primary School, Kennett

King Of The Sky

I live up mountains.
My feathers are black.
I love to eat other animals.
My beak is long and sharp.
I fly as high as a mountain.
My claws hold my prey.
What am I?

Answer: An eagle.

Henley Greenacre (6)
Kennett Primary School, Kennett

Colourful Feathers

I am as colourful as a rainbow.
My beak is for eating carrots.
My feet move quietly on the ground.
I have blue feathers.
I make a strange noise.
What am I?

Answer: A peacock.

Danielle Mission (5)
Kennett Primary School, Kennett

The Climber

I can jump really high.
I have a bushy tail.
I live in the tall trees.
I like to eat nuts.
I am as soft as a pillow.
I jump from tree to tree.
What am I?

Answer: A squirrel.

Emily Crysell (5)
Kennett Primary School, Kennett

Land Eater

I have lots of hair.
My tail is bushy.
I eat chickens.
I blend in with the trees.
Farmers hate me.
My fur is as fluffy as a T-shirt.
What am I?

Answer: A fox.

Harry Allison (5)
Kennett Primary School, Kennett

Sharp Claws

I am as soft as a pillow.
I have black stripes.
My roar is loud.
I have sharp claws.
I am as cute as a koala.
I love to eat meat.
What am I?

Answer: A tiger.

Chelsey Middleton (5)
Kennett Primary School, Kennett

Nut Eater

I am as soft as a pillow.
I am orange.
I eat nuts.
I have a bushy tail.
I squeak a lot and I like to eat lots all the time.
What am I?

Answer: A squirrel.

Thea Tucker (5)
Kennett Primary School, Kennett

The Scratch

I am a high flyer.
My home is made out of sticks.
I have a good grip.
I'm as fluffy as a pillow.
What am I?

Answer: An eagle.

Jack Jones (5)
Kennett Primary School, Kennett

Meat Eater

I have sharp claws.
My roar is as loud as a truck.
I eat meat.
I prowl in the long grass.
What am I?

Answer: A tiger.

Tristan Edward Taylor (5)
Kennett Primary School, Kennett

What Am I?

I am soft and furry.
I live in a house with my owner.
I like to eat fish and mice.
I can climb up a fence.
I have four long legs.
What am I?

Answer: A cat.

Benjamin Eldridge (6)
Walpole Cross Keys Primary School, King's Lynn

What Am I?

I am rainbow-coloured and wriggly.
I live in water with sharks.
I like to eat little fish.
I can swim.
I have fins.
What am I?

Answer: A fish.

Ella Mai Louise Ward (5)
Walpole Cross Keys Primary School, King's Lynn

What Am I?

I am orange and fluffy.
I live in a forest with bats.
I like to eat them.
I run fast.
I have a long tail.
What am I?

Answer: A fox.

Archie Munro (5)
Walpole Cross Keys Primary School, King's Lynn

What Am I?

I am brown.
I live in a house with people.
I like to eat bones.
I have four legs.
What am I?

Answer: A dog.

Krystian Vancans (5)
Walpole Cross Keys Primary School, King's Lynn

What Am I?

I roll in the mud.
I live in a sty.
I live on a farm.
What am I?

Answer: A pig.

Samuel Clements (7)
Walpole Cross Keys Primary School, King's Lynn

Slimy Slugs With Shells

I have antennae as sticky as glue.
I have a black, yellow and pink shell.
I have black, sticky antennae.
I am very small and very sticky.
I sleep in my shell.
My shell is cosy.
I have a shell on my back.
I walk slowly and make a trail of slime.
I live in my shell.
My head can go in my shell.
What am I?

Answer: A snail.

Eliza Rosemary Wilson-Bell (7)
Wells Next The Sea Primary And Nursery, Wells-Next-The-Sea

Deep Sea

I have two fins.
I am scaly.
I have a top fin.
I have sharp teeth.
I love to eat fish.
My teeth are as sharp as a dragon's.
I have a scratch on the side.
I live in the water.
I am white and brown.
My body is as slithery as a snake.
What am I?

Answer: A shark.

Ella-May Dawn Raven (6)
Wells Next The Sea Primary And Nursery, Wells-Next-The-Sea

Crazy Creature

I have pointy whiskers.
I have sharp teeth.
I am grey.
I have brown eyes.
I have furry legs.
I have a long tail.
I have pointy ears.
When you stroke me I might purr.
I have sharp claws.
I have a tail as long as a ruler.
What am I?

Answer: A cat.

Alisha Beckham (6)
Wells Next The Sea Primary And Nursery, Wells-Next-The-Sea

Fluffy Creatures

I have fine whiskers.
I have a soft tail.
I have a small body.
I have four legs.
I have a small neck.
I have a pink nose.
I purr quietly.
I have a soft, long and black body.
I have a pretty tail.
What am I?

Answer: A cat.

Lilly Andrews (6)
Wells Next The Sea Primary And Nursery, Wells-Next-The-Sea

Watch Out For Brown Fur

I have a soft tongue.
I have a black pupil.
I have a wet nose.
I am very tall.
I have sharp claws.
I have a long tail.
My paws are soft.
I don't live on ice.
I don't live underwater.
What am I?

Answer: A dog.

Kalei Dorothy Maisie Barnes (6)
Wells Next The Sea Primary And Nursery, Wells-Next-The-Sea

Look Out In Your House

I have a black, shiny nose.
I have four fluffy, long legs.
I have floppy ears.
I like to go on long walks.
I have yellow, golden fur.
I have a soft, waggly tail.
I have a loud bark.
What am I?

Answer: A dog.

Oska Somerton (6)
Wells Next The Sea Primary And Nursery, Wells-Next-The-Sea

Look Out For Wild Animals

I live in a zoo.
I have a long tail.
I am big.
I am stripy.
I have four legs.
I have big, long and stripy ears.
My roar is as loud as a bear.
What am I?

Answer: A tiger.

Edward Lees (7)
Wells Next The Sea Primary And Nursery, Wells-Next-The-Sea

Hopping In The Garden

I am cute, cuddly and nice.
I have cuddly, soft and ginger fur.
I am furry.
My fur is as soft as a cat.
I have long ears.
I have long whiskers.
What am I?

Answer: A bunny.

Ava-Jane Yaxley Beckham (6)
Wells Next The Sea Primary And Nursery, Wells-Next-The-Sea

Look For Fur

My tail is fluffy.
I have big and fiery eyes.
I live in a house.
My claws are sharp, very sharp.
I am soft and cuddly.
My eyes are creepy.
What am I?

Answer: A cat.

Ellie Duncan (6)
Wells Next The Sea Primary And Nursery, Wells-Next-The-Sea

I Live In The Zoo

I have stripes.
I love to eat meat.
I have sharp claws, as sharp as a knife.
I have a long tail.
I am hard.
I have lots of whiskers.
What am I?

Answer: A tiger.

Daisy Rustom (6)
Wells Next The Sea Primary And Nursery, Wells-Next-The-Sea

Look For Furry Creatures

I have a round head.
I have a long tail.
I have brown eyes.
I have sharp teeth.
I have a big tongue.
I have a white, soft, furry belly.
What am I?

Answer: A dog.

Zdennka Thomasine Gelder-Bailey (6)
Wells Next The Sea Primary And Nursery, Wells-Next-The-Sea

My Favourite Animal

I have short claws.
I am as fluffy as a cover.
My tongue is as big as Big Ben.
My skin is as fluffy as a cover.
My teeth are very sharp.
What am I?

Answer: A dog.

Tilly Boulter (6)
Wells Next The Sea Primary And Nursery, Wells-Next-The-Sea

Walking In The Park

I have sharp teeth.
I have a pink tongue.
I wag my tail.
I have a fluffy back.
I love my master.
I am Man's best friend.
What am I?

Answer: A dog.

Elise Honor Waajen (6)
Wells Next The Sea Primary And Nursery, Wells-Next-The-Sea

Swimming Animals

I have a long beak.
My wings are as long as a ruler.
People love me.
I love water.
I squawk.
I eat fish.
What am I?

Answer: A penguin.

Alfie George Thompson (6)
Wells Next The Sea Primary And Nursery, Wells-Next-The-Sea

Hop On The Ground

I have soft, fluffy fur.
My eyes are as small as a snowflake.
I have a short body.
I hop.
I have long whiskers.
What am I?

Answer: A bunny.

Isabelle Hayman (6)
Wells Next The Sea Primary And Nursery, Wells-Next-The-Sea

Swimming Animals

I have a wiggly walk.
I have a scruffy body.
I have a long beak.
I have a yellow, white and black body.
What am I?

Answer: A penguin.

Miguel Alexander Busque Pask (6)
Wells Next The Sea Primary And Nursery, Wells-Next-The-Sea

Under The Sea

I am scary.
I am huge.
I swim silently.
I eat meat.
I have gills.
I eat fish.
What am I?

Answer: A great white shark. (upside down)

Reece Steerment (6)
Wells Next The Sea Primary And Nursery, Wells-Next-The-Sea

Est.1991

YOUNG WRITERS INFORMATION

We hope you have enjoyed reading this book – and that you will continue to in the coming years.

If you're a young writer who enjoys reading and creative writing, or the parent of an enthusiastic poet or story writer, do visit our website **www.youngwriters.co.uk**. Here you will find free competitions, workshops and games, as well as recommended reads, a poetry glossary and our blog.

If you would like to order further copies of this book, or any of our other titles, then please give us a call or visit **www.youngwriters.co.uk**.

Young Writers
Remus House
Coltsfoot Drive
Peterborough
PE2 9BF
(01733) 890066
info@youngwriters.co.uk